I0829040

THE FOLLY AND COST OF DIPLOMACY.

SPEECH

OF

HON. S. S. COX,

OF

NEW YORK,

IN THE

HOUSE OF REPRESENTATIVES,

MAY 16, 1874.

"I am out of humanity's reach,
I must finish my journey alone;
Never hear the sweet music of speech,
I start at the sound of my own."
Supposed verses of Selkirk, by Cowper.

"The ocean which environs us is an emblem of our diplomacy, and the pilot and the minister are in similar circumstances. It seldom happens that either of them can steer a *direct course*, and they frequently arrive at their port by means which seem to carry them from it."—*Lord Bolingbroke.*

WASHINGTON:
1874.

SPEECH

OF

HON. S. S. COX.

Mr. COX. Mr. Chairman, I am well aware of the generosity and courtesy of my friend from Maryland who introduces this bill. It is a diplomatic arrangement, by which so eminent a democrat becomes its reputed father. There is no man in the House who can make a more graceful and dignified kow-tow before the head of the State Department and at the same time maintain his influence in this House. But, sir, I must be allowed to dissent from him on this matter.

The total amount appropriated by this bill is $3,347,304. There are amendments from my committee (Foreign Affairs) which would add $57,000 in one item; to say nothing of the increase incident to an adoption of the consular amendment. The bill will be over three and a half millions. Deducting the allowed claims of British subjects, which amount to $1,929,819, there is an excess of the appropriations of last year of over $150,000. Certainly the mysterious Brazilian item of $57,000 will be, must be, explained when we come to it in order.

INCREASE OF DIPLOMATIC APPROPRIATIONS.

It would be proper for me as a member of the opposition in challenging this bill to inquire why there has been such an increase in these appropriations from year to year. The reason of such an inquiry will be apparent when I say that whereas less than $1,000,000 very recently, sufficed for our foreign service, now we more than treble that sum! These items taken from the statutes are pertinent to my discussion:

Our diplomatic and consular expenses for the year ending June 30, 1859, were only $912,120; for the year ending June 30, 1860, they were $1,047,745; for the year ending June 30, 1861, they were $1,158,380; for the year ending June 30, 1862, they were $1,260,544.34; for the year ending June 30, 1863, they were $1,235,889.89; for the year ending June 30, 1864, they were $1,260,544.34; for the year ending June 30, 1865, they were $1,354,100; for the year ending June 30, 1870, they were $1,110,734; for the year ending June 30, 1871, they were $1,041,347. And now for this year, 1874, it bounds, like an India-rubber ball, high up to nearly three and a half millions!

I am sure that no one will claim special credit for the Department of State for the thorough thrashing we received in this city, from the British mixed commission award. We receive nothing, but we pay $1,929,819. The big bragging as to the Washington treaty requires much qualification when in the light of this item we consider how that treaty thundered its merits in the index and still rumbles in the air! After the extraordinary eulogy upon the State Department by the gentleman from Maryland, [Mr. SWANN,] I have been compelled to show the expenditures for other years—what our diplomacy used to cost, and how it has gradually grown.

THE SAVING SPIRIT.

By the platforms of all parties, we are reformers in matters of economy. All reforms at this time gladden the people. Every effort for economy calls forth their gratitude. Much commendation follows those who practice the saving spirit. Not a sigh would escape if half our ministers abroad, with their inordinate salaries and platitudinous dispatches, were abolished.

When one's household expenses overrun the income, is it not wise to stop gratuities to our relations outside of the household? Surely, we must be just before we are generous. Especially should we be just when there is little consideration received for the generosity.

My colleague [Mr. ELLIS H. ROBERTS] proposed the other day to suspend the rules with reference to this bill so as to change the title of the representatives of the United States to Portugal, Switzerland, Greece, Belgium, the Netherlands, Denmark, Sweden, Norway, and Turkey. He desired that these ministers should be envoys extraordinary and ministers plenipotentiary. He did not require increase of pay. O, no. This increase of *pseudo*-dignity does not mean an increase of salary, neither *in esse* nor *in futuro*. The House did not agree to his proposition. My friend from Indiana, [Mr. HOLMAN,] always vigilant, said it looked toward an increase of salaries, if not in this Congress then in the next. And he intimated what I have often urged, and sometimes with success, that we might have consular or commercial agents in the place of many of these useless ministers.

MERGING AND DISMISSAL OF MINISTERS.

As to many of these ministers named by my colleague, we might so combine their functions as to make one officer serve for many at a decreased cost to the Government. It is inconsequential whether we have any minister at Portugal or Switzerland. Certainly the minister at Constantinople might do the work also for Greece. Belgium might well be united with the Netherlands; and the Scandinavian countries, Sweden, Norway, and Denmark, should be merged in one embassy. Telegraph, steam, with their prompt communications; newspaper enterprise ever in advance of diplomatic dispatch; these and other elements of progress, have rendered ministers abroad trifling, expensive, and useless for every purpose of national comity, interest, or glory.

In this connection it might be well for me to say that the dismissal of many of our ministers abroad is no new thought. It is certainly not novel even to the English Legislature. May I be pardoned for referring to a debate in this House, in which I took some part?

On the 20th of February, 1872, in urging the union of the Central American missions, which carried, I said that "there were forty-five or fifty thousand dollars that could be saved without at all embarrassing the diplomatic service. I do not know but the nonsense, extravagance, and inutility of our diplomatic service is bringing us to the point to which the English government has been and is approaching. I mean the abolition of the whole diplomatic service. The Hansard Debates will show that in this age of steam and telegraphs, the English government, which rules the world of commerce, is considering how it may be rid of diplomatic business. It would have mere commercial agencies, or consuls, or special missions for the accomplishment of special purposes." (Globe, volume 88, page 1146.)

There has been no disadvantage to our country by reason of the merging of the Central American missions. It saved some $50,000, and it did no harm.

When we consider how distant our ministers are when they serve us, and therefore how irresponsible they become; how frivolous is their work and subservient and unrepublican their tone and habits, it is a shame to continue them, and it would be economy to dismiss them. If we had fewer irresponsible functionaries, local and foreign, we might better our interests and our position as a nation.

FOREIGN EXPERIENCES.

This idea of dispensing with foreign embassadors and, as I said in 1872, of remitting their business to commercial and consular agents, has been suggested not only by the progress of our age in international and material matters, but as the most amicable mode of closing complicated questions that might lead to war. Need I refer to special embassies? Need I refer to those of a commercial character, as that between France and England, when Cobden and Chevalier made the tariffs of two neighboring nations? Need I refer to the general congresses of European powers? Is it necessary to remind the House of the Ashburton treaty, or of the recent Washington treaty, as to which so much senseless eulogy has been pronounced? I venture to say that wherever there is a disagreeable complication that has in it a possible *casus belli*, there is likely to be a special commission to settle the vexed questions. The settlement of our northeastern as well as our northwestern boundary are evidences of this statement. In the English Parliament some of their wisest men have anticipated this advancement in the line of diplomatic obsoleteness. It has been proposed to disband the useless diplomatic retinue, and not without reason.

In 1870 Mr. Beaumont, in Parliament, said:

> If the whole system of diplomacy were done away with, and we had no permanent representatives in Western Europe, our peaceable relations with continental powers would suffer no interruption, and our commercial interests would be as well looked after as they are now.—*Hansard*, 199, page 550.

In 1860, speaking in Parliament, Mr. Labouchere said:

> There were a great many legations which with great advantage might be suppressed.

The Netherlands and Switzerland were instanced by him. He said further:

> He had been at a great many of those missions; he knew what was done in them; and he could assure the House that it was absolutely nothing. It was supposed that a minister did a great deal of good by asking important personages to dinner. * * He had asked a friend of his, who was minister at one of those legations, one time what he was doing; and the reply, "Doing? What do you think is to be done in such a place as this."—*Hansard*, 192, page 930.

If this be true as to Great Britain, which commands the commerce of the world, whose ministers and consulates, and whose gun and flag follow the sun in its revolution, then *a fortiori* it might be true of this country, which is so crippled in commerce and so limited in continental area and influence. More especially should it be true with reference to a country which does not or should not make its *salaam* before the kings and kaisers of the world, and which should not beg the favor which it cannot grant without humiliation.

It is no agreeable duty to refer to our retrogression in shipping and commerce. We know how we have lost and who does our work of transportation. We know how Great Britain has grown while we have lost. The relation which Great Britain bears to commerce for these periods I have before me in Palgrave's Notes on Banking, page 50. The imports and exports in 1819 are only £69,000,000 sterling;

in 1844, £144,000,000; in 1872, £603,000,000. The growth of France in spite of wars has been equally conspicuous. Compare our commerce, and the diplomatic expense which is supposed to be spent to foster and guard it! Then if you are content with your calculation, vote this and similar bills.

THE UTILITY OF OUR MINISTERS ABROAD.

Mr. Speaker, it is far from my purpose to dilate on the manner or character of appointments abroad; whether they be appointed for their intellectual or moral qualifications or for favor. The remark of Mr. Labouchere in Parliament adds fresh meaning applied to our appointees. It is perfectly well understood that in such affairs "kissing goes by favor." The favorites of the White House, or of the Department, or of Members and Senators, are the successful ones who see the world at the public expense. Political or partisan service thus hath its reward. An incompetent or unfragrant Cabinet officer, a defeated or *passé* Congressman, a vociferous stumper, or a potential editor, is the lucky man, regardless of his knowledge of foreign languages, of statistics, jurisprudence, or international law and customs. They do little harm, only because there are no opportunities; indeed, there is no opportunity for good either. A perusal of the volumes of our diplomatic correspondence (Executive Document No. 1, parts 1 and 3, of this Congress) will show the multifarious character of our embassadorial inutilities. One man writes home to glorify our arbitration with Great Britain, and another sends a package of public documents which the newspapers all have in advance.

The Austrian minister peddles scandal in dispatches against a Vienna commissioner, whom the President sends afterward to Japan and whom the Senate confirms. It is very gratifying to know from Brazil that the "Emperor is better, but cannot walk out yet;" to hear from Chili that Mr. Root, the minister, noticed an enormous whale disporting himself one morning near the tail end of this hemisphere, (page 111;) also that our "beloved President has endeared himself by recognizing our wild Indian as a brother man," (page 113;) that the Patagonians believe in two roads after death, one to the good and the other to the bad, preferring that to our religion. But why go over this voluminous correspondence? Much of it shows that our diplomats are not drones, as they work busily—at nothing. They have little or nothing of that employment which consists in making valuable treaties, or in that mystical equivocation which has made diplomacy the synonym of hypocrisy. It is only Mr. Bancroft, or some other minister, who in making treaties has gained for us the unenviable notoriety of unmaking citizens.

Besides, how few of our ministers really do the commercial work for what they claim and obtain credit. We vote $10,000, say, to send a minister to Paraguay. He never goes into Uruguay as is expected; but comes home to the stump, leaving a petty consul at Montevideo to do the work, while he inflicts on us at home his rhetoric and his consequence.

As this is a bill with some pretense in the way of economy, it might be well to compare our system of diplomatic economy with that of other nations. The State Department made its estimates for $3,688,524. This includes the printing of the "Diplomatic Correspondence" and "Commercial Relations." If we compare our economy with that of Great Britain, which has perhaps fourfold our relations with the world, commercial and otherwise, we find that we are the most extravagant of people with respect to our diplomacy.

The English estimates I find for 1873-'74 were £526,148—over

$2,500,000. The French appropriations are about the same as that of Great Britain.

As to France, I refer to the *Bulletin des Lois* for 1872, the most convenient authority, which shows that all the expenses of foreign affairs, including that of the department itself, amounted to only 11,883,500 francs, or nearly $2,400,000. And this law, unlike most of our laws, gives a detail of the expenses in a sort of exhibit. The great body of this expense was for the regular appropriations and the rest for what is called "*dépenses variables.*" This last is what we call a "contingent fund." Yet France, with all its continental relations and its traditionary relations, its necessity for keeping the peace amid continental foes, its complications as a propagandist through Europe and the world, and England, with all its extraordinary expenses, as the first and monopolizing commercial power, have an almost contemptibly cheap diplomatic system compared with ours!

How much more efficient they are than we. Where is our flag, (unless backed by other powers,) from the tropics to the poles, from the orient to the occident? Who gives heed to our claim for an outrage on our citizens or our flag? Who gave glory to Santiago? I do not say our ministers are worse trained, because they are politicians and partisans, than those of France or England. I scorn to refer to the traffic and professional work which our ministers abroad are accustomed to do.

I will not comment on the neutrality appropriation of $20,000 in the body of this bill. That bears its own comment. I have said so much on that and kindred topics, that some one might believe in this rude era that I was interested in something beyond the honor of my country.

Let us come down to something that will illustrate the wonderful utility of our diplomacy, for which we are asked three and a half millions. May I refer to the public documents now before the House to show how these millions are expended? May I contrast what they give us abroad? How timidly do our ships creep over the sea and wheedle and coax their way into ports; and how ignobly our citizens are thrust into prison, without redress and without reclamation. What, sir, is the value of our diplomacy to this land? Consider the way in which Mexico plays with us about our claims and the claims commission, breaking the treaty at pleasure.

Turn over those silly essays known as our diplomatic correspondence. Will our colored brothers look at Liberia first? It costs them something to keep up such wasteful officials. They pay for it when they buy a woolen suit or a hoe! What wonderful profundity is contained in the dispatches of our minister at that point! He has $4,000 per annum for his stuff. His confidential dispatches inform us that he has discovered by consultation that the coffee-tree is from six to seven years in attaining a mature growth. Goodness! Any encyclopedia tells us that. He does not know it even from personal inspection.

As a sample of the South America missions—that asylum of decayed and exiled patriots, go to Ecuador, where some man by the name of Rumsey Wing flies his embassadorial kite. He writes from Quito the day after the Fourth of July last—I hope it is because he celebrated the Fourth. [Laughter.]

QUITO, *July* 5.

HAM. FISH:

I have the pleasure to report to you, sir, that our national anniversary, sir, was generally observed, sir, in this city, sir. [Laughter.] I inclose dispatch.

I am, &c.,

RUMSEY WING.

Including exchange and contingencies Rumsey Wing's salary is $8,747 total, as per financial report for 1873, page 23. What a consideration for such information! Members will perhaps have observed a voluminous correspondence from a minister at Santiago by the name of Root. He is a doctor. Being thoroughly vaccinated he managed to catch the small-pox, got well easily, and turned his sanitary condition into the State Department. Although the press of Chili intimated that Mr. Root is radically wrong in intermeddling in their hospitals, yet I always forgive the physician when he has something to propose for the human race, especially in South America; for it is a sickly continent. In writing to Mr. Fish, he says that he performed the following remarkable marvel:

"I daily medicate great numbers by proxy." "My system of treatment is a great success." "The grand idea is to destroy the poison." "A new street has been named after me here." [Laughter.] "I generally prefer an enema rather than a purge; a favorite one is composed of oil of turpentine," &c. "In case of constipation, lemonade or other acidulated drinks." "I forward to the Department directions for a purge." [Laughter.] "When an alcoholic stimulant is indicated it should be one with as little acid as possible."

This gentleman has been considered the most remarkable plague in South America. Yet we pay for his performances, salary, exchange, and contingencies, over $11,000!

It would be impertinent for me to refer to a minister like Jay. He had an ancestor. He is very much like the bird of his name, in plumage and jabbering. His fume and fussiness in the Vienna matter is a simple scandal to our time and country. Let me skip these sedate, uniformed flunkeys of our ministerial system.

We come down to

ROMANTIC APPOINTEES.

This brings us to my friend Colonel Steinberger, and his report of the South Sea Islands. He is not a religious rover like Dr. Newman. [Laughter.] I think nobody will suspect him of being particularly pious. He is a scientist, a man of observation, rhetoric, and enterprise.

In all that I say I mean to support him as the proper candidate for the governorship of the distant islands which he has surveyed. He is suddenly called from his duties at Washington to the South Sea; why, no one can guess.

We are told by Shakespeare that—

On such a full sea are we now afloat;
And we must take the current when it serves,
Or lose our ventures.

I suppose that on this authority the colonel sails to the south pole. As Great Britain is now annexing the Friendly Isles, must we be idle? Why may we not seek for the Navigator's Isles? Thus our old jealousies are aroused.

A NEW SOUTH SEA BUBBLE.

Well, sir, my interest in these South Sea Isles does not come out of the bubbles of history which the English missionaries and John Law blew in the last century. It has a gentler fountain. I once knew a girl whom I traveled with in Africa, from the Grisons in Switzerland, who told me her grandmother had a lover along with Captain Cook in the good ship Endeavor, and was eaten in the Friendly Islands by the gentle savage! Hence my absorbing and romantic interest in those lands. [Laughter.]

But, Mr. Speaker, while I may have ideas inconsistent with those of my honorable friend [Mr. SWANN] as to the utility of the missions proposed by this bill, I think, as an old traveler into every continent, I ought not to object to the roving agents of the Department of State. The difference between them and myself is that I traveled at my own expense, and published my books at my own risk. Now, we have and vote a contingent fund. "Contingent" means depending on chance, *i. e.*, wherever there is a good chance to help a good gentleman of the church, like Dr. Newman, or a *chévalier d' industrie*, like Dr. Steinberger, we do it! Rev. Dr. Newman's observations are yet to be published. That good Methodist is now examining the Chinese wall for economical and architectural purposes. He will then skip over to the isle of Spitzbergen and describe the remarkable breed of dogs there, [laughter;] then flop into the equatorial regions, where—

Chimborazo stands sublime,
A land-mark on the sea of Time. [Laughter,]

Before the interest of his exploration inundates the moral and pious mind, let us take a glance at Colonel Steinberger. This gentleman was sent to the Samoan, or the Navigator's Isles. His report is Executive Document No. 45, Forty-third Congress, first session. Our committee has a recommendation based on his report for a commissioner to be appointed, with a good salary, to those isles. This is done with a view to a protectorate or annexation. Its discussion, therefore, involves his report, and gives it an emphasis not belonging wholly to science or journeying. We must vote on it. The "contingent" fund is at stake. In this is involved its proper use. The hardy granger and laborious artisan, the drowned-out planter and the honest miner, desire to know that their money has been well invested in the South Sea. In other words, let us observe the prisms of this new South Sea bubble.

For myself, I have borne my share of the expenditure with joy. It is not much. My share is about one-ninetieth part of a mill. Especially is this interesting in view of the fact that England has just annexed the Feejee Islands in that quarter of the globe, and appointed Captain Grover, an Ashantee hero, as its ruler.

WHERE ARE THE SAMOAN ISLES?

Where, then, are these isles? I thought I had a map. But I have been hurried into the debate to-day, and my friend from Maryland [Mr. SWANN] must have captured my missionary volume. No? [Laughter.] Some one has taken it, and hence I am embarrassed; but, Mr. Chairman, if I am called on in fancy to bound these isles, without my pious volume, [laughter,] I should point first to the isle of Juan Fernandez. Well, about eight thousand miles west just above the tropic of Capricorn, and forty degrees east of Australia, you will find them. [Laughter.] Robinson Crusoe was one of the nearest neighbors, and Botany Bay another. [Laughter.] The islands are considerably conducive to solitude, but not so much so as the isle of Crusoe. There are thirty-five thousand men and women of the Friday family on the islands. Already I seem to feel that we have annexed them. Contiguity of territory makes them so near in the light of humanity, yet so far, when we come to reflect. Cowper sang of Selkirk and his isle:

When I think of my own native land,
In a moment I seem to be there;
But alas! recollection at hand,
Soon hurries me back to despair.

I can only travel to these distant coralline shoals in these pages of the gallant colonel.

But how, sir, shall we bound them? On the north by the aurora borealis? [Laughter.] On the east by sunrise? On the south by the south pole? On the west by——

A Voice. By Sunset. [Laughter.]

Mr. COX. That is personal. No. By the Day of Judgment? Yes, that will do, as the map does so isolate them. They are situated in the midst of an inexpressible watery waste. They are, to be accurte, seventy-two hundred miles from Juan Fernandez, [laughter,] the same distance from San Francisco, and the same distance from Loo-Choo, and the same from the seat of the Acheanwar. What charms has this comparative solitude for our Crusoes of civilization. It is for these isles that the farmer burns his untransported corn in Illinois; for these the drayman or truckman "pays his shot" and starves in the eastern city. It is for these isles, to be acquired with a contingent fund, that the artisan labors and strikes in New England; and that the colored laborer, who picks cotton in the South, sickens to see, to love, and to annex. 'Regardless of expense he would like to see this quarter of a million of money for a contingent fund go out to the antipodes.

The rest of my speech will be in explanation of this remarkable fact. I know that I can only *half* tell it, and moieties always need an explanation.

It was not enough for the Administration to make an attempt on San Domingo. Failing in that they now reach out to the Polynesian group. That group is noted as having had in it the Botany Bay of England; ay, and within a few months, a recusant French democrat, Rochefort, escaped from one of the French islands by swimming through one mile of sharks. This illustrates the vigor of democracy against the ravenous shoal which lives to destroy.

OUR COMMISSIONER STARTS.

By an order of President Grant, Mr. A. B. Steinberger was appointed in March, 1873, special agent to visit and report upon these Samoan islands. The President was not satisfied with the juvenile romance entitled "The Swiss Family Robinson," [laughter;] nor with Robinson Crusoe, with his dog, parrot, and man Friday, so interesting as a clever story for youth, by a persecuted Dissenter. He was not content with the various reports made by the missionaries from the Friendly and other adjacent islands. Captain Cook was to him a myth; and the men who ate other men were no less a myth.

A pilot-boat, called the Fanny, is chartered under the "contingent fund." It sails from San Francisco in June, 1873. But alas! for such expeditions! The San Francisco press anticipates it, and when our embassador reaches the Sandwich Islands, to use his own language, he assures "His Majesty King Lunalilo that he is in nowise accredited to his government, and that newsvenders in this as in many other cases are irresponsible agitators." The reporters' gallery will take notice and tremble!

In August, our commissioner reaches the eastern island of the Samoan group. The islands are called "Navigators" because, as our commissioner says, navigators have alway avoided them, [laughter,] just as the Friendly Islands are called friendly because everybody was eaten when they went there. This group which we seek to annex consists of nine islands.

As the question becomes one of economy in an appropriation of money, in order to impress the House against the appropriation I have thought of using three rhetorical modes: First, the scientific; second, the pietistic; and third, the simplicity of my ownstyle.

SCIENTIFIC VIEW OF THE ISLES.

In order to develop the scientific view, I would say, irrespective of what our commissioner has said, that while there are evidences of craters in these islands, there are found ancient vesicular lava and amygdaloids, the olivine often disintegrated, and mountains of basaltic rock, against which the great swell of the ocean breaks with deafening roar. This will readily be understood by the House, [laughter,] and especially by the gentleman from Ohio, near me, [Mr. GARFIELD,] whose voice has in it many pleasant, if not deafening, associations. [Laughter.]

Leaving for one moment the report of our commissioner, I would add that there are found there, in the circumjacent waters, round masses of mæandrina and astræa, contrasted with delicate leaf-like and cup-shaped expansions of explanaria, and with an infinite variety of branching madreporæ and seriatoporæ; some with mere finger-shaped projections, others with large branching stems, and others again exhibiting an elegant assemblage of interlacing twigs of the most exquisite workmanship. Their colors are unrivaled, vivid greens contrasting with more sober browns and yellows, mingled with rich shades of purple from pale pink to deep blue. Bright red, yellow, and peach-colored mulliporæ clothe those masses that are dead, mingled with beautiful, pearly flakes of eschara and retepora, the latter looking like lace-work in ivory. In among the branches of the corals, like birds among trees, float many beautiful fish, radiant with metallic greens or crimsons, or fantastically banded with black and yellow stripes. Patches of clear white sand are seen here and there for the floor, with dark hollows and recesses beneath overhanging masses and ledges. These bright creatures have not always peaceful lives. There are many kinds of sea animals that have holes in the corals, and take up their lodgings among them, while some kinds of fish prey upon them. I presume this is a political parable. [Laughter.]

This will answer for the physical description. As a resort for coral, these island are a success. But why did not our commissioner describe in scientific phrase how the sweet little Simians, (ordinarily called monkeys,) [laughter,] with the prehensile grip of the extended *os coccyx*, swing from the *Callophyllum inophyllum*, in the sunshine upon the upper slopes of Upolu and Savaii? [Laughter.] As they swing some eight thousand miles from us, and as a Darwinian, and a friend of man and science, why should we hinder them? Let them swing! [Great laughter.]

Still we should not complain, for has not our commissioner given us the yellow *Artocarpus* or bread-fruit tree, and the *Cocos nucifera* or cocoa-nut which the intelligent monkey drops upon the head of the juvenile islander?

SAMOANS AS CHRISTIANS.

The pietistic interest connected with these islands dates almost as early as Captain Cook's voyages. The first Sabbath spent in this land by the missionaries is memorable for a sermon, in English, from the words: "Behold, I am the Lord, the God of all flesh: is there anything too hard for me?" (Jeremiah, xxxii. 27.) [Laughter.] The natives who understood little of the language, believing that all mankind were of one flesh, seized, cooked, and consumed the missionaries. [Laughter.] They found them too hard for digestion, and were shortly after converted.

In handsome style, and at our expense, Colonel Steinberger relates the present pious condition of the natives. On page 21 of his report he shows that in 1869, when a religious census was taken, there were 35,107 of all religions; Independents, Presbyterians, Wesleyans, and Catholics. This makes a majority of 504 more religious people in the island than there are population. [Laughter.] It is therefore a fair inference that everybody on the island belongs to some Christian persuasion. It is safe to say that there is not a single Samoan who has not accepted Christianity, though more devout and zealous in some districts than in others.

DAN AND JIMMY.

Aside from the missionary enterprises, it might be well to state, in the language of the commissioner, how this remarkable acquisition to the Christian religion took place. He says:

Williams found, in 1830, that the natives knew something of Christianity, and readily accepted it. This knowledge evidently came from the rude teachings or influence of castaway sailors, as the natives still speak of the white men among them long before the arrival of missionaries. Of such was "Dan the Convict," who captured a vessel, the Roma, murdered the captain, burned the ship, and landed in Savaii. He could neither read nor write, yet taught the natives, through their superstition. Such another was "Jimmy the Sweet," who regularly preached to them. Many interesting stories are related of these characters by the natives. [Laughter.]

It may be necessary to recall the fact that "Dan the Convict," who was a pirate and murderer, and "Jimmy the Sweet" likely came from Saint Giles and the Old Bailey. [Laughter.] Their mode of propagating the Christian system must have been peculiar. How did they produce such a remarkable effect upon these simple South Sea islanders? Perhaps they related how Peter denied the Lord, the rooster crowed, [laughter,] and induced all the islanders to copy Peter's example. [Laughter.] Or perhaps, following the text from Jeremiah, they taught them the necessity of consuming the missionaries without grace, in order to be full of the holy unction. [Laughter.] Perhaps the story of Judas impressed them. Evidently "Jimmy the Sweet" and "Dan the Convict" left their impress upon these islands, which our Administration desires to annex. They pointed to the cross and to the impenitent thief. [Laughter.] I can well imagine what sermons they could have preached to these heathens. Did they teach them to pray for their daily bread, with the bread-fruit tree, as our commissioner says, hanging around their houses? What a meaningless, wasteful excess of prayer, even for a South Sea islander!

SAMOAN MUSIC.

What songs did they sing? If I had before me the volume edited by a Miss Farmer, on the missionary history—but my friend [Mr. SWANN] who has urged this bill has doubtless purloined this volume, [laughter,] and still withholds it in my direst need—then I could show to the House, a picture of natives sitting in a ring round the missionary, either "Dan the Convict" or "Jimmy the Sweet." [Laughter.] Near by the waves of the ocean lave the shore. The rude hut, surmounted by the cocoanut and the banyan tree, the bread-fruit and the palm, speak to us so touchingly. Each native sits squat, upon his sacred mat. The hymn is given out and lined. I had the music of that hymn in the volume referred to, and which my honorable friend continues to withhold. [Laughter.] Captain Wilkes heard the same refrain. Its meaning is "Thanks," "Good evening," "How are you?" "Is your mother well?" [laughter,] &c. Beautiful salutations from Polynesian lyres! The language is "lelei," "leleei." I am inclined to ask my friend [Mr. SWANN] to join me in the song. [Laughter.] His voice would add to the music. [Laughter.] It is much the same as I have heard in the drawling songs of the barbarians of the South

Mediterranean coast. Captain Cook, when he first heard it, said it was not entirely disagreeable. But the historian says that the captain was in a good humor that day. Delicious odors filled the air, and he had drunk high and full of the kava-bowl, and the music seemed not to be discordant. Yet our commissioner says in his report, from which I quote, that the Samoans are fond of music without melody. [Laughter.] In church and school each child seems to outvie the other in vocal power and compass, [laughter;] that the instrumental music is confined to the beating of sticks upon mats and hollow logs. What kind of music this may be which exalts their pious enthusiasm is hard to determine. As a comely concordance is often helped by a convenient discord, even as affection is made more intense by disagreement; so when we annex this music of the Polynesian Pacific to that of the Atlantic—when it is accompanied by such prime donne as Nillson, Lucca, and Di Murska, the effect would be unexampled. [Laughter.] When to the rich, intwisting golden threads of the grand organ of the minster, vibrating and swelling through gothic aisles, you add from these isles of the Southern Sea those dissonances which are recorded and set to music in this missionary volume, it would not be unlike adding to the lyric gush of the Stabat Mater, or to the mighty feather of the "Messiah," a roundelay from filing a New Hampshire saw on a frosty morning, or a refrain from an overloaded and underfed donkey. [Laughter.]

To what sentiment should this Polynesian music respond? Ah! I understand it. By some preconception, they would sing from Watts—

And are we rebels yet alive,
And do we yet rebel,
'Tis wondrous, 'tis amazing grace,
That we are out of hell! *

[Laughter.]

POLYGAMY.

How far they have been converted to Christianity so as to be fit subjects for our rule may be learned further from the commissioner's report, from which I quote: "Polygamy is common on the part of men, never on the part of women; two wives seldom live in the same house; a plurality of wives is not common, the husband usually sending his wife to her people when he takes a new one. Virtue in Samoa is predominant.* The maiden of a village is reverenced more as a virgin than as a chief's daughter." So that when the House of Representatives shall vote the proposition of Secretary Fish for cordial relations and perhaps annexation of these islands to our country, I feel like calling the roll of gentlemen who voted the other day to investi-

*A word of apology is required in this revised edition. The missing missionary volume has appeared. My friend from Maryland is acquitted. But the music of the isles, for which we must pay our money, is unreported by our gallant commissioner. One or two staves will answer as a sample. I take it from Sarah Farmer's volume on "Tonga and the Friendly Islands," page 43.

gate the heinous polygamy of Utah. And may I not ask that a commission be sent to Samoa before we annex?

WAR.

To show further the remarkable Christian principle of these islands, let us look at their manner of conducting war. Is not war a fair test of allegiance to the Prince of Peace? As to this, says the commissioner, "the Samoans are patient, earnest, easily controlled by their leader. While cruel to their enemies, they are never treacherous. Prisoners are never taken. The importance of a victory is measured by the number of heads taken. [Laughter.] The head is publicly exposed and reviled; but never mutilated." This would seem to give a refinement to war to which our Modocs have never attained. Our Indians are actuated by the same refinement to take not only the scalp of a hairy but of a bald-headed man. No one escapes; but they only take the scalp. These Christian Arcadians in the South Sea Islands, whom we would annex under the orders of the Secretary of State, are never satisfied without having the whole head! [Laughter.] I do not refer, as an evidence of Christianity, to the diseases prevalent in their midst. I might refer to the protuberances which surgeons are compelled to cut from the bodies of these self-indulgent islanders. The subject, however, is too nice for this delicate Congress. Besides there are diseases—elephantiasis, soriasis, &c.—which characterize these islanders. Before we annex them, it might be well to state that elephantiasis is not any disease connected with the *Pachydermata*, but it is a swelled leg; while soriasis is nothing more than the itch. This, however, is no special objection to annexation with our Administration. [Laughter.]

THEIR DRESS.

If I referred, as the commissioner does, to their disposition to assume the dress of the whites—the white gloves, silk dresses, enormous crinoline, paniers, old-style bonnets for their May meetings—some one might say that I was making points against our revolutionary ancestors and ancestresses, who, as we were informed the other day, dressed in such *outre* habiliments.

LEGAL-TENDER "MATS."

It would be well, perhaps, in considering the financial condition of our country to quote from the commissioner with respect to the "sacred mats" produced there; not because they are sacred, but because they are regarded as a legal tender. Our commissioner says, on page 24, "that families count their wealth, and all personal and real estate is computed by 'fine mats.'" "For the secure establishment," says our commissioner," and maintenance of a home and foreign government in Samoa, the hereditary and fictitious value of 'fine mats' must be destroyed. This could best be done by affixing a Government stamp and making them a circulating medium subject to redemption, as is paper money." Was there ever so easy a solution of our troublesome problem? Besides giving us a fixed standard, it would energize and encourage a new branch of industry. It is especially encouraging and protective, as it is some seventy-two hundred miles from us! [Laughter.]

Why not, then, send for the chief of Pago-Pago to settle our distressing questions of finance upon the principle of fine mats and redemption? And yet, on page 41, the commissioner says of the natives of those islands, "In theory they display some wisdom, but they must fail in practice. They fully realize that some government must aid." Let us rush to their assistance. They are only 7,200 miles off! [Laughter.] Leaving, therefore, the report of the commissioner, and going to the appendix, it gives me a great deal of pleasure to say that our commissioner to Mauga, the chief of Pago-Pago, recognizes the intelligence and the financial supremacy of the United States, for this chief writes to President Grant that "his (the chief's) people are poor, and his finances are less; that the good teachers have taught us to be honest, observe your doctrine, and maintain your faith." What a satire on American legislation, after our legislation on polygamy and the President's veto!

Further, the chief says, if *he* himself ever said it at all: "We know you are a great people, with many ships and many warriors; that you are all united in peace."

This chief of Pago-Pago had not heard of our failures to revive shipping, or of Louisiana and reconstruction; South Carolina and taxation; and Brooks and Baxter were as unknown to him as Castor and Pollux. [Laughter.] He says to President Grant: "We know that you cultivate the soil and build great houses." He had our grangers and architects in his mind. [Laughter.] He says "You make great roads." He had a dim intimation of Credit Mobilier. [Laughter.] He says "You talk to each other through the air." He had in mind Congress, and perhaps the remarkable speech of my friend, [Mr. SWANN,] who still insists on withholding my pious missionary volume. [Laughter.] Or perhaps he had in mind the marvelous talk of the telegraph. He says "We want the same; and pray for aid and protection and friendship from the President of the United States." God help him! Poor simple Arcadian! He says "We are poor; but we are happy in our peaceful condition." Why, sir, should Colonel Steinberger disturb that felicity? Why did not they eat him, even if they could not digest?

OUR RED-MEN.

The second appendix to this remarkable report is a letter written from Pago-Pago in 1873 to this great chief, Mauga, by our commissioner. He tells the chief that he was impressed with the Christian character of the people he visited. Not even a nail was missing from his ship when he left the Samoan country. "In our country," says the commissioner to the great chief, "we have many tribes of natives, (referring to our Indians,) but they are not so peaceable or honest as yourselves." This was said before Shacknasty Jim or Captain Jack had succumbed to our military forces. "Only a few of these natives are Christians," he said. He could say that with truth. I look about me for my gallant friend from Indiana, (General SHANKS,) to verify this remark. [Laughter.] Where is he?

A MEMBER. Here he is.

Mr. COX. Let him learn from what I shall read, what our commissioner told the Samoan chief and what the United States Government gives our red men. It gives lands, farmers, tools, teachers, clothing, and provisions, besides making laws for them. These remarks will commend themselves to the chairman of the Indian Committee, as well as to General SHANKS. The recent appropriations on Indian business have their finest commentary in this simple statement of our commissioner to the chief of Pago-Pago.

But why should I go through this whole report? Is it not enough to satisfy the hard-working people of this country that their money is well invested, that a "contingent fund" should always be applied to the furtherance of our projects for annexing the South Sea Islands?

FEMALE DISTILLATION.

Nay, I have omitted one thing we need; we seek for revenue and economy. The females of these islands are an incarnate distillery. [Laughter.] No crusaders disturb their operations. There is a beautiful spreading shrub called the *Macropipii Methysticum*, the root of a kind of pepper-plant, a delightful soporific, properly administered, but through the abuses of men it has been transformed into an intoxicating beverage. Our commissioner says that he has seen no case of stupefaction or intoxication resulting from its use. How is it prepared, and in case of annexation how can we recover the internal-revenue tax?

Our commissioner says that the liquor is prepared from the dried root by a process of mastication by young girls, and strained through cocoa-nut fibres into a large bowl, hewn from the trunk of a tree. These young virginal distilleries "must be healthy, with sound, clean, teeth." [Laughter.] According to another authority which I have before me, the root must be bitten carefully while in the mouth, with little moisture mixing with it. Then it is prepared for the Samoan festivity.* Captain Cook had a saturnalia with this remarkable liquor; and I am not sure but his final death was occasioned by a too free indulgence. One thing is sure, that never since the time of Spenser's Fairy Bower of Bliss, when his beauteous heroines pressed the grape between their pinky fingers, could it ever be said with truth that "So fair a wine-press made the wine more sweet."

Who that admires the beauty of the Samoan woman described by our commissioner, as having eyes black, soft, and pleasing, with melancholy air and meekness, with skin of polished copper, proud in bearing smooth, straight, erect, and symmetrical, including the tatooing so well pictured in this report, would be reluctant to drink the wine of so fair a wine-press? Where are your burgundies, sherries, clarets, champagnes, mantillados, and lachrymæ christæ—compared with this Samoan liquor! Let Lucullus dash the gemmed goblet from his luxurious board; let Bacchus reel under the burden of his vine-leaves and his bibulous excesses. Let Longfellow tune his lyre in praise of Longworth; let him chant, like an inspired Silenus, the praises of the creamy Verzenay. What are these to the original vintage of the Samoan Islands. No wonder women crusade against those liquors which are—

Drugged in their juice
For foreign use,
When shipped o'er the reeling Atlantic,
To rack our brains
With the fever pains
That have driven the old world frantic: [Laughter.]

Let them annex Samoa, and pray no more.

Yet, Mr. Speaker, why should we annex these islands? Some harsh and crabbed person like my friend from Indiana [Mr. HOLMAN] or my friend from Vermont [Mr. WILLARD] will ask me why we want so distant and so extravagant a relation. Perhaps I am peculiar. We can have nothing worse than we now have. Almost anything would be better. It was Josh Billings who remarked:

I never owned a kammel-leopard yet, and hope I shan't; but if I shold hav to take one in payment ov a det, I shood konsider I had lost the det twice. [Laughter.]

Perhaps he had this sort of acquisition in his eyes.

CUBA AND CIVIL RIGHTS.

Before entering upon the enormous travel and acquisition contemplated by this report, would it not be well to inquire why it is, when called upon to protect and annex such a people, thirty-five thousand strong, in the South Sea antipodes, some seventy-two thou-

* Sarah Farmer's Tonga, pages 48, 49.

sand miles afar, [laughter,] that we do not protect and enlarge into the light of liberty the thousands who are in slavery near us, on the island of Cuba? It might also be well to consider, when we have so many local and domestic questions connected with our Indian and other colored races, growing out of their desire to live and to be buried equally with the whites, why their status is not fixed somehow, before we recognize and organize another race. Certainly our interests with Cuba involve in many ways our economies, not merely as to luxuries like cigars, but as to the necessaries like sugar. It involves the liberty of a race which made our civil war and cost us seven billions of money and a million of men. But I am growing serious. I meant only to present the best side of this remarkable foreign affair.

REASONS PRO AND CON FOR ANNEXATION.

When we consider the relative distances of these Samoan isles from our shores, and the fact that earthquakes and volcanoes have so abounded therein that the patient work of billions of coral has been distributed by the premature appearance of basalt and granite, it is clear that it comes within the limited powers of our Federal Government! Moreover, when we remember that our Bureaus are examining into our own faunæ and floræ—that we are making the Yosemite and Yellowstone, Parks and tributary to science by Federal exploration and publication; when even our Capitol is decorated with the birds and beasts and creeping things of our hemisphere; and as these matters are defended as within the purview of Federal authority—who does not rejoice in the discovery by our commissioner of the spotted snake that crows and the extinct dodo, which, like the phœnix and the griffin, are delivered from the unknown realms of fancy! Sir John Mandeville and Munchausen are not, for reasons unnecessary to rehearse, fit for publication by a veracious Administration, but the luminous and unpleasant truths of this pamphlet are indispensable to Federal legislation and the average intelligence. For instance, we have long been discussing finances with their inflations and contractions. What a ray of light is cast upon these abstruse subjects by the discussion of our commissioner of the sacred mats!

Many reasons might be urged for the acquisition of these isles. Not because perpetual summer there simmers in the sunny air; not because bread-fruit is produced without planting, plowing, harrowing, or reaping; not because the cocoa gives from the fruitful bosom of mother earth its milk for young and old; not because our commissioner has discovered, as he thinks, the dodo—[Laughter]——

A MEMBER. Tell us of that bird.

Mr. COX. I reserve the dodo. [Laughter.] Not because polygamy there prevails and Christianity sings its hymns in discordant monotone; not because it recognizes caste and has "mats" for legal tender; not because it adopts the discarded toilettes of our civilized dames and demoiselles; but because the thirty-five thousand *indigènes* will, when annexed, become consumers of our products; and when they buy our hatchets and nails, our whisky and tobacco, our hair-pins and hoop-skirts, our hymn-books and bibles, will we not in this time of distress here add to our revenues? Hence, I am for Mr. Fish's proposition. Not, however, do I favor it on mercenary grounds! O, no. When Mark Twain received from the Persian Pasha his picture set in diamonds, he exclaimed, "O, sire, I do not care for the setting. It is only the portrait I crave." [Laughter.]

Neither, sir, is it because I would have a convenient isle of refuge for those who may leave us in 1876. [Laughter.] The good men who are as careful as they are honest in administration, the men of moieties and the Indian contractors, might find in these isles a happy refuge and resting-place, free from the persecutions of a venal press and the indictments of indignant grand juries.

Mr. Speaker, finding a contingent fund of $231,000 in this bill; knowing what contingencies are and how they grow and go; knowing the needs of the Treasury which is bankrupt, and the needs of the people who have to make up the deficiency, I should be derelict in my duty if I did not insist that we should cut off the large body of this expense growing out of our foreign relations in order to draw to us the polygamous and Christian and commercial people who live so many thousands of miles away from us; who are so near and yet so far.

I think, Mr. Speaker, these remarks will illustrate the remarkable comity, patriotism, and expeditions of the State Department. May their worst endeavors be better than that of San Domingo, and their best tend to the interest and honor of our country.

To conclude, Mr. Speaker: In these remarks I do not mean, by word or gesture, to extenuate or exagerate the delinquencies of our foreign department. Whenever I can see that my Government defends the Flag, recognizes and protects my fellow-citizens abroad, does not yield its rights and interests to a foreign potentate, and holds aloft the scale equity, of it will be my pride and pleasure to support ond defend it. During the civil war I never failed in that respect. In the coming years, if I shall serve here, I shall be more than usually observant of all those rules of comity which command respect from the world by granting and demanding justice. But may I not ask that such exhibitions of American enterprise as I have commented upon, for which we pay $213,000 contingent, and for islands so many thousand miles away, may become less frequent, and thereby save us from national humiliation?

O

www.ingramcontent.com/pod-product-compliance
Lightning Source LLC
LaVergne TN
LVHW011147110826
845150LV00008B/2566

* 9 7 8 1 4 1 8 1 9 1 7 4 0 *